Why Progressives Should Support Donald Trump

Michael Greshen

I'm grateful for the help and support of my family in writing this book. I want to thank my wife, above all, whose editing and typesetting of the manuscript was instumental. I also want to thank my mother for helping to improve the book with her thoughts and feedback.

Any errors are solely my responsibility.

CONTENTS

This book is the independent work of the author and has no association whatsoever with the Trump campaign.

If the premise of this book seems absurd to you, it's hardly surprising. Listening to the media and their soundbites, I couldn't have imagined I would ever write a book like this when I heard some of the things Donald Trump was saying. There's really no denying that, for progressives like myself, at least, he has uttered what is truly some of the most offensive rhetoric ever to come out of any political candidate!

That's why it was such a shock to me when I dug deeper and found myself agreeing on issue after issue with Trump's positions once I set aside my instinctive hatred for his offensive, politically incorrect rhetoric and looked at what he was really advocating. I also began to respect both his intellect in presenting issues in a way that was politically palatable to conservatives and his integrity in maintaining positions that, while unpopular, seemed to me to be solidly on the side of the American working class.

It first occurred to me that I should maybe give this blustery billionaire another chance when I read that he had previously considered running for President on the Reform Party ticket in 2000, and had also been a registered Democrat as well. With his talk initially of not wanting to rule out a run as a third-party candidate and the attacks that were being orchestrated against him at the highest levels of the Republican Party, it was becoming clear that he was not part of the GOP machine.

As I began to read what he had written and said and the positions he had taken, Trump's willingness to say things that were outside the Republican orthodoxy – and often very much in line with my own progressive thinking – began to impress me more and more. While I harbor no illusions that Donald Trump is a progressive candidate in the sense of a Ralph Nader or a Dennis Kucinich, some of his positions would not be entirely out of line in the platform of either candidate, for example, universal health care.

But what most impressed me was his ability to

sell an end to interventionist wars and the unending parade of military entanglements to the GOP base. Yes, he did it in what was a repugnant way to us progressives, positioning himself as the undisputed toughest candidate on the very real threat of terror. But in doing so, he has accomplished something that none of our peace marches nor our support for Obama and the Democrats has ever been able to accomplish: he (with no small help from the Obama administration) has finally galvanized conservatives against what I consider to be nothing less than the ongoing genocide of peaceful, non-terrorist Muslims in countries like Iraq, Syria, Libya and elsewhere.

Trump is also not beholden – nor should America be – to the countries that have revealed themselves to be the most regressive in terms of human rights and are themselves the biggest supporters of terror. Saudi Arabia comes instantly to mind.

As a self-financed candidate, Trump can take positions like this and follow through on them in a way that Bush and Obama could not, because he can afford to refuse special interest money, even all the way through the general election. He is free to be a true public servant and focus on running America as a successful businessperson would. I would not have written this book if I didn't believe he has the best interests of this country at heart – and by that I mean the interests of the honest working people of this country, not its hedge funds and foreign creditors. Trump will be able to act on behalf of those interests in a way that no Hillary Clinton or even a Bernie Sanders would.

While I'd like to begin the book by addressing the most obvious problems progressives have with Trump's candidacy, specifically his rhetoric on Islam and immigration, I think it's important to first confront the current situation we find ourselves in without any illusions. If the world really were the way it is portrayed in the mainstream media, where everyone is united against terror and the government has never done anything underhanded nor ever carried out a war under false pretenses, then sure, I would continue to vote for the Democrats as I have in the past. But as George W. Bush has so eloquently spoken: if we get fooled again, shame on us.

I am aware that the arguments I'm making in a book like this might well end up being used against Mr. Trump in the Republican primary. Establishment GOP outlets like the *National Review* have already taken exactly this line of attack, labeling Trump a pro-choice liberal and the like, and we can expect more of the same from his rivals. I would not be surprised if there are many on both sides who will disagree with what I've written, and I certainly welcome a healthy debate.

I very strongly doubt, however, that my impassioned plea for progressives to take another look at Trump (and a candid look at their own candidates) is going to be the thing that finally supplies the mainstream media with the kryptonite they need to counter his amply tested Teflon personality.

I've tried to write from the heart, let the chips fall where they may.

THE TRUTH ABOUT OBAMA
AND THE CLINTONS

When I voted for Obama in 2008, it was an ecstatic time. I was so proud of our country for rallying behind the peace candidate. More than once I found myself listening to his speeches with tears in my eyes. When he stepped into the Oval Office, it seemed so certain that our country had left a dark and dangerous time behind and we were headed into a bright, peaceful future of cooperation and an end to the pointless wars that had killed so many and squandered our country's reputation.

But the first signs that it was not to be so came quickly: more than a few heads turned when Obama kept on Bush's Secretary of Defense, Robert Gates. Then, when Obama appointed Hillary Clinton Secretary of State, many wondered why they had worked so hard to elect Obama over Clinton – most of us purely because we preferred Obama on foreign policy issues – when he then immediately put Clinton in charge of our foreign affairs.

But I continued to give Obama and his administration the benefit of the doubt, and I voted for him again in 2012. I defended him against the criticism of other fellow progressives who pointed out his failure to follow the agenda he had been elected to carry out. Nobody was happier than I was when the announcement of the death of Osama bin Laden came across the airwaves – finally, I thought, the wars and the killing are going to end. Obama is finally going to bring about the enduring peace the Nobel Prize Committee and we progressives were so sure would rain down from the heavens and into our parched throats, dying of thirst for an end to needless war, as a result of his ascension to the Office of President.

Unfortunately, this was not to be the case. To my own very deep embarrassment and that of many progressives who supported Obama, the President began to push for war and regime change in new theaters. To those of us who had spent years scrutinizing the Bush administration's agonizing wars of aggression that made so little sense, the list of countries in which Obama and Clinton began to pursue regime change through covert and overt means sounded alarmingly familiar.

I still remember vividly the shockwave that ran through the activist community when General Wesley Clark appeared on stage with *Democracy Now*'s Amy Goodman, recounting his meeting with top Pentagon brass only *ten days* after the 9/11 terrorist attacks:

> *One of the generals called me in and he said, "Sir, you gotta come in, you gotta come in and talk to me a second.' … He says, "We've made the decision. We're going to war with Iraq." This was on or about the 20th of September.*
>
> *I said, "We're going to war with Iraq? **Why?**" He said, "I don't know!" He said, "I guess they don't know what else to do."*
>
> *So I said, "Well, did they find some information connecting Saddam to al-Qaeda?" He said, "No, no, there's nothing new that way, they just made the decision to go to war with Iraq." He said, "I guess it's like, we don't know what to do about terrorists, but we got a good military and we can take down governments." So I came back to see him a few weeks later and by that time we were bombing in Afghanistan and I said, "Are we still going to war with Iraq?" and he said, "Oh, it's worse than that!"*
>
> *He reached over on his desk and he picked up a piece of paper and he said, "I just got this down*

from upstairs," meaning the Secretary of Defense's office, "today."

And he said, "This is a memo that describes how we're gonna take out seven countries in five years, starting with Iraq and then Syria, Lebanon, Libya, Somalia, Sudan and finishing off, Iran."

It's hard to describe the sinking feeling we anti-war progressives felt when Obama began to call for an invasion of Syria in August of 2013 – two years after regime change in Libya had plunged that country into chaos and handed it over to radical Islamic terrorists on a silver platter. Although Obama's push for war was rebuffed by Congress officially, unofficially a covert war was begun anyway. A covert war with a dark side that included a strategic alliance with radical Islamic terrorists.

Suddenly, we began to hear the strangest rumblings from Washington, D.C. – al-Qaeda had somehow become "moderate"? We were "accidentally" equipping ISIS with all the vehicles and weapons it needed? The accidents were becoming a little too routine, and the news began to take on a "theatre of the absurd" quality, as ISIS fighters paraded around with all their shiny new American equipment, and in now-infamous photos, riding in a pickup truck bearing the logo of a very unlucky Texas plumber.

Once Russia entered the fray and did far more

damage to ISIS in a few days than the US had done in over a year of war carried out under the pretense of fighting the terrorist group, it became impossible to ignore the facts. I remember discussing with a group of friends – we felt it honestly had begun to seem like Vladimir Putin might be the only one in the world left who could put a stop the machinations of a rogue Obama administration that had apparently forgotten which side it was on.

Because, we all reluctantly agreed, we voters evidently have zero power to stop the needless wars. We can elect the Nobel Peace Prize winner and still end up with just a seamless continuation of our worst fears about the Bush administration – simultaneously supporting or even creating terrorists while carrying out duplicitous wars of aggression using the subterfuge of combating the terrorists who somehow always managed to outsmart our fighting forces. The "unintentional" equipping and sheltering of ISIS by the US and its allies mirrors the Bush administration's "airlift of evil" in Afghanistan that spirited the Taliban and al-Qaeda forces away, just as our brave soldiers closed in, making a mockery of the War on Terror once again.

* * *

The shameful and disgusting continuation and initiation of war after pointless war and the deception of the American people it entails, although it is for me and for many progressives the central issue of our time, is hardly the only issue on which the Obama administration has betrayed the progressive cause and, in my opinion, the American people.

Obama has also betrayed the American worker on trade, much to the benefit of China, further eroding what's left of our job base. The tragic situation led even Democratic member of Congress Sherrod Brown (D-Ohio) to complain:

> *When we cause them to lose their jobs, what kind of self-government is that? What does that say about morals? . . . That our government can do something that causes all this trade dislocation and economic dislocation, our workers lose their jobs, and we say, 'Sorry, can't do anything for you'? (Huffington Post, 5/20/2015)*

The Trans-Pacific Partnership (TPP), long kept a secret from the American people, was "even worse" than critics like Bernie Sanders had imagined, while Hillary Clinton was quick to straddle both sides of the debate, being for it and then against it. Like Republicans, whose grand strategist Henry Kissinger was dubbed "China's single best lobbyist" by the *New York Times*, every move the Obama administration makes on trade somehow manages to end up as a victory for the People's Republic of China.

This pattern we have become all too familiar with is worse than the betrayal of America by one party or another, it is the collusion of *both* parties to *consistently* and *continuously* betray America, regardless of who is in office. While I have no doubt there are any number of honest, hard-working individuals in government at lower levels, at the level of the presidency we have been sold down the river by slick marketing campaigns that massage our consciences into submission.

This is hardly a new phenomenon: I am old enough to remember President Bill Clinton's betrayal of unions and the working class with the passage of NAFTA and GATT and the establishment of the World Trade Organization (WTO), which we progressives protested in vain in Seattle in 1999.

It is with a heavy heart that I am forced to admit that the election of Barack Obama we worked so hard for, far from bringing the "hope" and "change" we were promised, was merely a public relations upgrade for the same neoconservative/neoliberal agenda that the Clinton and Bush White Houses carried out.

Is there any progressive activist who hasn't felt the steel of Democrat betrayal stab them in the back?

Rep. Barney Frank, supposedly a leading progressive in the Democratic Party, has revealed himself to be a wolf in sheep's clothing when it comes to banker bailouts and banking reform, and more recently, even penned an article entitled "Why Progressives Shouldn't Support Bernie."

Yes, Barney Frank, you and the Democrats are the main reason why we progressives shouldn't support Bernie Sanders, because you will make sure he never has a chance. The (repressive) tolerance of his campaign functions to channel progressive activists' energy into safe spaces that have no chance of affecting the two-party duopoly and to give a certain air of legitimacy to Hillary Clinton's campaign through Sanders' inevitable endorsement of her candidacy, something which we progressives have seen coming many, many miles away.

Luckily for us, and for America, there is another option.

ISLAM, ISIS AND TERRORISM

Donald Trump's candidacy has come to be defined by one single statement more than any other, and it's his own fault. "Donald J. Trump is calling for a total and complete shutdown of Muslims entering the United States until our country's representatives can figure out what the hell is going on" was the text of the prepared third-person statement Trump delivered in South Carolina on December 7th, 2015.

To progressives like myself, it's a ridiculous and Islamophobic statement on its face, and his rivals on both sides seized on what seemed like the biggest gaffe to emerge from any campaign in recent memory. But, instead of sinking the Trump luxury yacht, he rode the wave of popularity the statement brought to undeniable front-runner status in the GOP race – no other candidate approaches his support in the polls as I write this, three weeks after the public has had time to digest the statement.

It would certainly be easy to do as nearly all progressives have, to take a quick swipe at Donald and those 'idiot' Republicans on Facebook or Twitter and congratulate ourselves on our politically correct perfection as Bernie Sanders-supporting Obama voters with a celebratory microbrew.

As progressives who attempt to live up to the biblical precepts our conservative brethren claim to uphold, we have spent a great deal of time "loving our enemy" after the attacks of September 11th. We have fought Islamophobia and war at every turn, we've prayed with Muslims, we've attended interfaith gatherings, we've given to charities to help those hurt by our nation's wars, we've studied Arabic and the Qur'an and we have taken the side of the oppressed Muslim in every case. Many of us, myself included, have come to understand Islam as potentially a progressive, liberating religion, one which gave birth to the humanist values of the Enlightenment and which saw its ultimate flowering in the light of

Islamic Spain broken on the wheel of Christian Europe's barbaric Dark Ages and the Spanish Inquisition.

But let's step outside the controlled media narrative of universal condemnation and labeling for just a moment and apply the "love your enemies" standard from the Sermon on the Mount to our "enemy" Donald J. Trump, as well. And, if I may risk the ire of the atheists among us, let's apply another of Jesus' precepts from the Sermon on the Mount while we're at it, and remove the beam from our own eyes before we attack the speck we may see in Mr. Trump's.

* * *

We progressives have been complicit in the genocide of Muslims in Iraq, Syria, Afghanistan and in many other countries, and we have to take responsibility for our failure. We've directed our efforts into avenues that have allowed us to "feel cool" and be popular, to be accepted socially and to be politically correct in the public sphere, but we haven't been effective. We've been divisive. We've been accusatory. We've been harsh, we've been shrill, we've been unloving and insulting. We've fought with each other and allowed ourselves to be divided and to be cowed. We've given up. We've rested on our laurels. We've been complacent and comfortable, and we've put our own comforts, our families, our jobs, our reputations above the lives that are being taken in our name.

Yes, we can make excuses: we were lied to by the media, we were taken out of context, our efforts were sabotaged. But at the end of the day, playing the blame game doesn't change the fact that we have been and continue to be unable to prevent illegal wars that amount to mass murder in our name, and history will judge us for it.

We've also done some remarkable things, and the election of Obama is still something we should be proud of, even though it has resulted in new wars of aggression, wars that may yet lead to World War III, because we came together for a candidate who was offering us the peace we had been working for. Intention has to count for something. But heaven help us if we fail to recognize the chance we have right now to come together with conservatives and support the only anti-war candidate in modern history who might actually have the freedom to act according to his own moral compass.

While Trump has taken some heat from the conservative establishment for positions that he has held in the past that are more liberal than his present positions, his opposition to the many wars carried out by Republicans and Democrats alike has never wavered.

In the most recent Republican debate, Trump channeled the thoughts of every American who has had to come to terms with the incredible cost of our miserable wars, responding to a question from Wolf Blitzer about whether or not the world would be better off if some of the dictators America had toppled were still in power:

> *In my opinion, we've spent four trillion dollars trying to topple various people that, frankly, if [these dictators] were [still] there and if we could have spent that four trillion dollars in the United States to fix our roads, our bridges, and all of the other problems, our airports and all of the other problems we had, we would have been a lot better off, I can tell you that right now.*
>
> *We have done a tremendous disservice not only to the Middle East, we've done a tremendous disservice to humanity, the people that have been killed, the people that have been wiped away, and for **what?** It's not like we had victory. It's a mess. The Middle East is totally destabilized, a total and complete mess. I wish we had the four trillion dollars, or five trillion dollars. I wish it was spent right here in the United States on our schools, hospitals, roads, airports and everything else, that are all falling apart.*

Despite the hearty applause from the GOP debate audience in Las Vegas, Carly Fiorina immediately cut him down for daring to utter such a moving condemnation of the Bush-Obama wars. "Wow, that is exactly what President Obama said," she chided him over the audience's cheering. While she may be right – what Trump had the nerve to say as the GOP frontrunner was very similar to the impassioned arguments we heard from Obama that won him the election – there is a big difference. If Trump is elected, we won't be electing another marionette of a thousand special interest puppet-masters who will be putting far different words into his mouth once in office.

How does Donald Trump get away with this? How does he continue to brush off attacks from the right? It's simple. Trump has positioned himself as the strongest anti-terror candidate, he has done it in a way that resonates tremendously with his conservative base, and he did it in the most effective way possible: in an offensive soundbite that was *guaranteed* to cut through the media chatter like a hot knife through butter. There's nothing disingenuous about it – he is genuinely the strongest anti-terror candidate. Trump was talking about the threat of terrorism long before it became *de rigueur*. In his 2000 book, *The America We Deserve*, Trump devotes an entire chapter (and then some) to convincing us to take the threat of terrorism seriously, invoking his uncle John Trump's warning that the country was vulnerable to a mass casualty terrorist attack on a major American city.

You can say what you want about Donald

J. Trump, but I don't think you can argue that he is unintelligent. He's playing to win, and he has just solidified the conservative base around him in a way that will protect him from the continuing attacks of the pro-war establishment right.

In case you haven't noticed, conservatives in America have been engaging in the most despicable Islamophobic rhetoric imaginable. I hardly need to cite any examples, but if you do feel that you need a quick refresher course in the level of anti-Muslim bigotry that has become the new normal for many in this country, simply visit the comments section on any YouTube video having anything to do with Islam. Many conservatives view Islam as a monolithic evil and believe very much that we are locked in a "clash of civilizations" between the forces of good and evil. For someone with this mindset, Trump has connected with them in a way that no other candidate will be able to.

He is now free to disengage from the unnecessary global militarism and genocide agenda that has dominated post-9/11 bipartisan foreign policy, and instead to focus on what we all agree should be the first priority, the *defense* of America against those who would threaten her people.

I am willing to look past this very calculated anti-Muslim remark for one reason alone: I believe it may well be the necessary manure that will fertilize the tree that will bear the fruit of peace. We have become so focused on rhetoric in this country, on political correctness, and it's absurd when we know that our politicians do the opposite of what they say, day in, day out. That's basically their job description; they do it for hire. But if we force ourselves to confront the reality that we and our government have been carrying out a genocide while proclaiming our innocence by launching a public relations salvo of pro-Islamic "religion of peace" platitudes, let's take ourselves down a couple of notches, get off our high horses and start to wrap our snobby little heads around the fact that Trump might just be able to accomplish what we could never do – make our nation a defensive promoter of peace instead of an offensive aggressor at war.

It's embarrassing to think how much of my own life has been wasted pursuing exactly this goal of trying to convince conservatives – to no avail – of the logic of peace. Like Spock's "old Vulcan proverb" from *Star Trek VI*, "only Nixon could go to China," I'm asking you to at least entertain the possibility that only a Trump can end the wars.

Peace is not a partisan issue. Richard Nixon was elected as the peace candidate who had a "secret plan" to end the war in Vietnam that Johnson had escalated.

Unfortunately Nixon's betrayal of his constituency, his expansion of the Vietnam War into Laos and Cambodia, mirrors Obama's own broadening of the wars that he was elected to end into Syria, Libya and elsewhere.

* * *

Whatever the real geopolitical reasons for the Iraq War may have been (beyond enriching shareholders of Halliburton and the rest of the military-industrial complex) remains unclear. Evidently the Iraq War wasn't, as many progressive activists like myself believed, "blood for oil," because we haven't shown much interest in the oil, which, as Trump himself correctly notes, has ended up in Chinese hands. Were we spreading democracy? Did the Bush administration actually believe their own WMD lies? Was it simply the Cheney one-percent doctrine in action? Or did it have more to do with initiating a series of wars that ultimately leads to war with Iran? We may never know.

One of Hillary Clinton's standard talking points has become her praise of George W. Bush for saying that Islam is a peaceful religion and that the United States is not at war with Islam. These two Islamic scholars seem to come from the same school of Islamic jurisprudence. Unfortunately they come from the same school on another issue as well. Clinton supported the Bush administration's push for war in Iraq, and even the normally uncritical Bernie Sanders has blamed her for the rise of ISIS:

> *She was proud to have been involved in regime change in Libya, with [Muammar] Gaddafi, without worrying, I think, about what happened the day after and the kind of instability and the rise of ISIS that we have seen in Libya. (London Guardian interview, Dec. 18, 2015)*

Whether or not we are at war with Islam is debatable, but one thing is certain. If we set aside the false rhetoric coming from the White House and the media and look at the reality of our Syrian strategy in which ISIS plays a key role opposing the moderate dictator Assad, if we look at our nation's unflinching support for Saudi Arabia, if we look at our founding of al-Qaeda in the 1970s, if we look at the Muslim schoolchildren who would become the Taliban who were taught militant Islam using textbooks provided by the US, it is clear that we have *not* been at war with radical Islam. In fact we have been nurturing its growth for quite some time.

This ultimate betrayal of the American people – to ask us to go to war under false pretenses and to act as al-Qaeda's air force while innocent families are killed, tortured and maimed – is what our contributions to Obama's campaign have ultimately bought us. They have also brought us to the brink of a World War III scenario with Russia. If you feel that's consistent with your values as a progressive, if you feel that's money well spent and you want to do it all over again with Ms. Clinton, then you and I have a vastly different moral compass.

When Clinton calls Donald Trump the "ISIS candidate," the irony is astonishing. Clinton is, unless she has been nothing but a passive puppet of the President as Secretary of State (which certainly seems unlikely), the Obama official most responsible for the rise of ISIS, as she was in charge of our foreign affairs at the time when it occurred.

Quite tellingly, Clinton herself blamed Obama's failure to act militarily in Syria for the rise of ISIS in an August, 2014 interview with *The Atlantic*, stating:

> *The failure to help build up a credible fighting force of the people who were the originators of the protests against Assad—there were Islamists, there were secularists, there was everything in the middle—the failure to do that left a big vacuum, which the jihadists have now filled.*

It's unclear how toppling Assad would not simply have left a bigger vacuum, of course, but the most striking thing about this statement is her position that the President should have gone to war over the objections of Congress and the American people.

Her statement clearly dissembles on at least two levels. One, Clinton is openly advocating arming Islamists as a means of combatting ISIS, when it is clear that ISIS shares personnel and weapons with many other Islamist and non-Islamist groups. Two, she is posturing as if this hadn't been done, when clearly this is exactly the strategy that was pursued, although the extent to which the US was arming radical Islamic terrorists was obviously not supposed to be public knowledge.

But on a deeper level, Clinton is telling the truth, albeit in a way that ascribes agency to the wrong party. The failure of the US to carry out regime change in Syria using conventional warfare *is* what led to the Obama administration's strategy of equipping the terrorist army in its proxy war against the Syrian government with only a paper-thin veneer of deniability.

And Hillary Clinton now wants us to vote for her precisely *because* she would have gone to war in Syria without hesitation, *on the side of al-Qaeda* and other so-called "moderate" rebels, *regardless* of what Congress or the American people wanted. She would have dragged us, kicking and screaming, down Rumsfeld's yellow brick road of death, and now claims this qualifies her to be the responsible, progressive candidate whom we should now trust to fight ISIS over a "dangerous" Trump. Does this sound like someone who learned their lesson from the "mistake" of supporting the Iraq War? Does this sound like the progressive candidate to you? More importantly, are you going to conveniently forget about these facts when the media does and vote in a Clinton administration whose knee-jerk foreign policy impulse is regime change?

Donald Trump has been far more consistent in opposing regime change even than Bernie Sanders, who said in an October 3, 2015 interview with the *Washington Post*:

> *I support President Obama's efforts to combat ISIS in Syria while at the same time supporting those in that country trying to remove the brutal dictatorship of Bashar Assad.*

Sanders' adoption of the war machine's schizophrenic lie shows that he resides in the same neoconservative fantasyland as Bush, Obama and Ms. Clinton, where the US can magically transform whatever glaring untruth into any reality it chooses, so long as it serves the all-important goal of a perpetually expanding war of aggression.

This is nothing new – Sanders also supported the war in Kosovo in 1999, which Donald Trump opposed.

And although Bernie Sanders frequently touts his one major anti-war credential, having voted against the war in Iraq, he had no problem voting to fund that war once it began, nor did he shy away from supporting regime change in Ukraine. He has performed his job in Congress admirably: his role seems to have been to subvert the efforts of the many dedicated progressive activists of Vermont – and now he's punking the entire progressive wing of the Democratic Party.

* * *

Of course Trump is no pacifist. He has vowed to hunt down terrorists, and unlike the present administration, which simply makes a show of fighting terror and somehow manages to continue to "accidentally" equip and supply ISIS even as Russia exposes the entire fiasco on the world stage, I believe he may actually do it. But what he will avoid, and what America must avoid, is the constant regime change and destabilization that we've been engaged in without interruption during both the Bush and Obama administrations.

Regime change is not making us safer, and when we hear Hillary Clinton claiming that ISIS is using Donald Trump videos for recruiting tools – well, she would know. ISIS has been one of her many covert methods of undermining the Assad and Gaddafi regimes. If you want to know how to recruit ISIS fighters, I couldn't think of a better person to ask for advice.

If you're comfortable with a Democratic Party whose function is to make you feel cool while carrying out raw, bloody mass murder of Muslim civilians – and many Christians as well – while supporting the terrorists they claim to be fighting, then of course it is your right. But take a look at the rivers of blood on your hands before you accuse Trump of being a racist for saying the one thing that could stop the slaughter of Muslims by an out-of-control war machine. Because I can tell you without a doubt that Hillary is not going to put the brakes on the massive industry of death that has backed her from the beginning.

Even now, we hear rumblings from the Republicans about running a third-party candidate if Trump wins the primary. Maybe a Jeb Bush? He and his family seem to have a very particular way with swing state voting machines, if not with the voters themselves.

Trump is not part of the script, and incredibly, he's winning. This is not at all what the elite have been expecting and the establishment's rage is palpable. He's managed to unite the GOP base around a focus on terrorism and immigration, but as he has himself said, he is "no warmonger." Trump is quite simply pro-America, and it's been far too long since we've had a president who puts this country first, who doesn't have the messianic desire to burn up America's wealth and its military as fuel for a globalist regime change agenda.

Take a look at the "new American century," because it's already here, and what Obama has effectively done with his Nobel Peace Prize is carry the neocon torch further into the darkness of defeat.

I wish there was some way to effectively communicate the suffering of a people. I wish I could make you taste the deaths we've caused, I wish I could flip a switch or choose a certain phrase that would let you know and feel the atrocities we progressives have been responsible for. Our failures should be written in blood on our very souls.

How can Americans, who should be the best informed citizens in the world, be so delusional about their own role in it? How many have we killed? Can we still just say "oops" when it happens the tenth, the twentieth time? Or is our ignorance as "willful" as Obama's protection of the Islamic State terrorists?

IMMIGRATION AND THE
RESERVE ARMY OF THE UNEMPLOYED

Karl Marx may not exactly be the most popular thinker in America, and certainly not the one you would expect me to invoke in support of the very capitalist Donald Trump. But Marx may well have been right when, in 1845, he said that "the ideas of the ruling class are in every epoch the ruling ideas, i.e., the class which is the ruling material force of society, is at the same time its ruling intellectual force."

Could this be why we are living in a stifling intellectual environment in which personal attacks of racism are at a fever pitch, an atmosphere in which a stilted political correctness has replaced genuine concern for the other? Why are our media obsessed with the reification of race? Does racial tension benefit the "ruling class" of our time?

While these larger questions aren't going to be resolved here, there is at least one issue where it's quite clear where the interests of the ruling elite capitalist class in America lie: with the division of the working class into races in conflict with one another.

If I may be permitted one more paradoxical invocation of Marx in a book advocating support for Donald Trump without endangering the very fabric of the universe, there is another important concept I'd like to bring up: *the reserve army of the unemployed.*

Let's consider what Marx said. We all know where his ideas about solutions have led and it's not good, but some of his basic observations about the nature of capitalism are spot-on. And if the Democratic Party were, in fact, representing the interests of the working class, we might hear logic like this a little more often:

> *The primary goal of the ruling class with respect to the worker is, above all, to obtain the commodity of labor as inexpensively as possible, which is only possible when the supply of this commodity is as large as possible in relation to the demand for it, i.e., when as much overpopulation*

as possible occurs.

Instead of protecting the standard of living for working Americans, all we hear from the Democratic Party, in lockstep with a media who makes sure their name-calling "resonates," are accusations of racism leveled against anyone who dares to point out the obvious implications of increasing illegal immigration for wages and unemployment. The Democrats know which side their bread is buttered on, and the media is there to help them if they forget.

Not that Republicans have done any better on this issue by the American worker, despite the fact that this is one issue their party base really cares about. If the function of the Democratic Party is to carry out the pro-war agenda while proclaiming peace and love to deceive their constituents, then the function of the Republican Party is to undercut the working class and drive down wages through increasingly unrestricted immigration and other means while campaigning on the notion that they care about "border security" and "jobs."

In reality, both parties are beholden to corporate interests who demand lower wages and are not afraid to accuse you, the American worker, of being racist if you oppose their plan to profit at your expense. They collude to spend our tax dollars rolling out the red carpet for anyone who wants to volunteer for their army of undocumented, unprotected, extremely underpaid workers and help them lay off less underpaid workers.

As progressives, of course we feel sorry for the impoverished Latin American underclass coming to America seeking a better life, and we feel responsible for their plight due to American corporations' unconscionable exploitation of them, often enforced by dictators or even US troops at the barrel of a gun. *This* guilt that we feel and the accompanying racial tension, unlike the guilt we *should* be feeling for the mass murders carried under the false pretense of fighting ISIS out by our progressive champion, Barack Obama, is *very* useful to the wealthy elite of this country and is therefore encouraged.

This particular guilt for centuries of oppression of the Americas is cultivated, exploited, and utilized against us all, regardless of race, and what's much worse, it's most harmful to those among us with the least means, regardless again of whatever racial category they would like us to identify with. They divide and conquer the labor market in a very cynical strategy that serves to lower wages for Americans who have to compete at the bottom of the pay scale, all to assuage the guilt of middle-class Americans who may pay no personal price due to illegal immigration and may even themselves benefit by hiring an undocumented worker or simply by hiring someone whose wages have been driven down in competition with undocumented workers.

Is it any wonder then, that social activism, the activism that "resonates" in the media at least, has been reduced to a petty, micro-level politics of personal racial identity? Sociology programs across the country have gone from teaching that there is no biological basis for racial categories and that we should look beyond them, to being the biggest promoters of racial categorization, forcing our students to think of every social interaction in racial terms and accept that many of them are inherently racist due to their "whiteness." This ultimate perversion of political correctness into a Nazi-like racial classification system purports to have, as its goal, an end to "white privilege."

But the message of these scholars of white privilege resonates in the media, and therefore among students conditioned by it, for two very important reasons: first, their skin-deep micro-analysis handily avoids any questions of social structure or political policy, which is ideal for a media who loves a witch-hunt but can't allow any change to occur that threatens the status quo. These one-trick academic ponies who limit their analysis to the level of rhetorical and then levy their carefully crafted ad hominem racial argument onto it are a match made in heaven for a media who faces the same restrictions against delving too deeply into the actual nature of social problems that transcend sensational accusations of racism. They have developed an intellectual scaffolding, a template that leaves no room for counter-argument, which allows for fantastic personal attacks of racism to be erected on the flimsiest of foundations, essentially on the basis on an individual's "whiteness," their perspective and contribution to society is rendered null and void. Any action other than acquiescence to whatever it is the accuser wants the accused to do is now automatically racist. Q.E.D.

The second reason the application of this racial lens has proven to be a gravy train for academics and journalists alike is that not only does it decenter systems and institutions as the unit of analysis, not only does it help to divide a working class against itself along racial lines, but most importantly, it coincides with a media master narrative in which any critics of the Obama administration can be handily dismissed with the simple use, perhaps even just a hint, of the 'racist' label. It is the propagandist's ultimate ad hominem weapon to shut down all discussion and simply label whomever is presenting unwelcome facts or views with the pejorative "racist."

The pseudo-academic perspective that offers the power-brokers in Washington and their media lackeys a blanket application of the racist label to all whites, to the entire Republican party and, in general, anyone who opposes any aspect of the Obama agenda, is well worth the salaries earned by these predominantly white, supposedly progressive scholars of race who have conspired to shut down actual inquiry into social justice issues from a humanist (rather than a racist) perspective. "Check your privilege" is a coded racial euphemism for "shut up, you have no right to express your opinion because of your race."

The irony of the entire "white privilege" movement is that, at least in academic circles, it is these predominantly white scholars of race who are filling positions studying racial discrimination that could have gone to African Americans, Hispanics, or other marginalized groups who might not be so focused on name-calling and labeling, who might be more aware of the threat such a re-introduction of racial categories (as if they are somehow real again) poses. Are we supposed to return to "separate but equal" to satisfy the egos of a clique whose "activism" seems all but custom-made for government and corporate propaganda?

Of course, white privilege does exist, but a renewed focus on racially dividing America is hardly the way to go about eliminating it. And there are lots of intersecting privileges – including the privileges liberals derive from going along with their corporate paymasters' agenda – that somehow fail to make the evening news. And far be it from me to criticize movements that are trying to make the world a better place – there have been far too many police shootings and there has been far too much killing at home and abroad, and I applaud anyone standing up for their rights and against such a system. But the media and the academy have allowed a sensational drive for ratings and acceptance to cloud their judgment, and they advance in their careers by helping big corporate employers flog this "race" horse all the way to the bank.

It's amazing how liberal our government can be with taxpayer money when they find a cause or a group who serves their agenda. While food stamps are no longer available for poor Americans without children, and the funding just doesn't seem to be there when Obamacare forces businesses to cut low-wage workers' hours and the most impoverished suffer, there is a seemingly endless amount of funding to help illegal immigrants once they enter our country. Constantly we hear that Social Security is going to have to be cut for our nation's seniors, but there are plenty of free bus tickets to anywhere for undocumented workers. And the gravy train doesn't end there.

It's easy to see who controls the purse strings,

and it's not the American worker. They would love to be able to brand anyone who opposes their agenda to destroy the income-producing capability of the average American worker a racist, and self-promoting activists and academics have handed them all the ammunition they need.

There's a very selfish argument we often hear being made by the mouthpieces of the elite and those who have bought into their racializing of the labor issue – the argument that undocumented workers "do jobs that Americans won't do." That just doesn't hold water. Do we have such a surplus of jobs in this country that we can not only afford to be choosy, but that we have to provide financial support for immigrants who enter the country illegally just to stem the flood of all these extra jobs nobody wants?

We progressives are well aware of the long history of racism in our immigration system, historically biased quotas etc., and of racism toward immigrants themselves. Many immigrant groups have faced racial discrimination in this country, and it's hardly the proudest moment in our history. Of course, it's easy to find examples of openly racist anti-immigrant rhetoric still today.

But that doesn't mean that we cannot advocate limiting immigration to those entering the country legally without automatically being racist ourselves.

While there are those who would argue that Trump has no right to speak on the issue because he is white and therefore automatically racist using the reasoning I've outlined above, somehow remaining completely unaware of the irony inherent in what they're saying, the opposing side is also not immune to charges of *systemic* racism. Is it somehow *less* racist to advocate firing or at the very least paying poor US citizens who are disproportionately from minority backgrounds less for their work by bringing in illegal immigrants to compete with them? Should we jettison all the workplace and wage protections generations have struggled to provide for the American worker? That doesn't sound like a very progressive rallying cry to me.

* * *

The media uses our fear of being labeled racist against us, to get us to act against our own interests and most especially against the interests of the poorest working Americans, whose blood, sweat and tears are so vital to corporate America's bottom line. They are using race, like any other wedge issue they can get their hands on, to divide us and to prevent us from being able to unite around our common interests.

Now, I'm not saying electing Trump as our next

president is going to fix everything overnight. But it's time to put our own need to feel the sense of belonging that comes from sharing in the abuse of a scapegoat aside, to examine where those motives are coming from and if they really benefit the groups we're told we're helping, and realize that we can stand up for the American working poor and not sell them down the river – without automatically being a racist. Even if we do happen to be pigment-impaired.

And as for the whole concept of race, let's face the facts. It was a dumb idea. But the elite have gotten far too much mileage from it to let it go so easily. Of course we all have different cultural backgrounds, but the idea that our interests diverge because of the color of our skin or what countries our ancestors came from is a weapon we cannot afford to hand to those who would use it as a wedge to divide us politically in order to conquer us economically.

WOMEN'S RIGHTS

The media has bombarded us with criticism of Donald Trump for making disparaging comments about women, making fun of their looks, and for making derogatory, sexist statements. They accuse him of acting like a male chauvinist. It's not difficult to find this type of soundbite – "The Donald" readily gives the media the red meat they need, and in so doing he continues to dominate the news cycle. In some cases, not all, it does honestly seem that critics' interpretations of his comments are over-reaching and off-base, but I'm not going to try to defend each of his comments or split hairs over interpretations, because I think there are far bigger issues at stake for women and girls in this election.

Besides, Donald Trump has certainly never made any statements anywhere nearly as derogatory toward women as those made by Senator Bernie Sanders. In 1972, Sanders published an essay in a zine called the *Vermont Freeman* that began with the following passage (and I really should warn the reader at this point that this is not exactly something you want to read aloud to your children):

> *A man goes home and masturbates his typical fantasy. A woman on her knees, a woman tied up, a woman abused.*
> *A woman enjoys intercourse with her man – as she fantasizes being raped by 3 men simultaneously.*

Sanders' article explains further his philosophy about sexual violence and rape, about how "women adapt themselves to fill the needs of men, and men adapt themselves to the needs of women," i.e. to be abusive rapists, to be the aggressive, abusive partner that women need, to satisfy what Sanders calls women's "qualities of dependency, subservience and masochism."

To be fair, he is somewhat vaguely calling for people to rise above it, but everything Sanders writes in the essay makes the central point that sexual abuse and rape are as natural to the man as are being raped and abused for the woman, that these are the normal sexual roles and that deviating from them seems impossible.

"Do you know why the newspapers with the articles like 'Girl 12 raped by 14 men' sell so well?" Sanders asks, rhetorically. He gives nonspecific credit to women for "trying to pull themselves together" – a backhanded compliment, or just some obscure 70s lingo? – but ultimately, he concludes, "Men and women – both are losers."

I can feel my progressive self wanting to make excuses for him, but I know in my heart that's just the "us vs. them" mentality – the same one that makes it so easy for us to glom onto every single concocted smear against Donald Trump without thinking twice.

Although the media generally hasn't hesitated to repeat charges of sexist language being made against Trump, the cases often don't really seem to be very clear-cut. Usually the attacks depend on a particular interpretation being read into a word like "wherever" or "that," interpretations which may or may not reflect his supposed veiled thoughts. My own feeling is that at least in some cases, it is clear to an unbiased judge that Trump wasn't actually intending the entendres that have been attributed to him.

Listening to his tone of voice when he speaks of

Fox News anchor Megyn Kelly going after him viciously in the debates, for example, when Trump says she has "blood coming out of her eyes, blood coming out of her wherever," it doesn't sound to me like he is hinting at any innuendo. He doesn't emphasize the word 'wherever' that commentators have made so much ado about, which suggests to me that his explanation of what he said, that he was maybe going to say "nose" or "ears" but abandoned the metaphor as it didn't seem to be working very well, is in fact true. I don't hear anything in his voice that suggests he is trying to get us to think of something in particular with the use of the word "wherever." It really sounds for all the world like he is trailing off on one idea and moving on to take a new tack.

It's less clear to me whether or not we should give Trump the benefit of the doubt for a comment he made about Carly Fiorina's appearance to a reporter writing for *Rolling Stone*. Because we are unable to listen to his original comments, but only see them their printed form as the reporter alleges them to have been made, it becomes a bit of a case of he-said-she-said, since Trump denies that he was talking about her actual face, but rather her persona. In an interview with Greta Susteren, he did seem to backpedal a little on that and say that he made those comments as an "entertainer," essentially arguing he was 'in character' similar to his role on *The*

Apprentice at the time he made the comments.

But it's not like he said women just want to be tied up and raped. Imagine – if Bernie Sanders becomes president, is he going to legalize rape? Will he reclassify sexual assault as a just another sexual orientation? Will sexual assault defendants begin to raise the "Sanders defense"? "Your honor, given that all women really want is to be brutally raped and beaten by gangs of men and since all men want this too, hey, I'm just doing what comes natural. You're not some kind of respectful monogamous psychopath, are you?" Donald Trump has never said anything even remotely like what Bernie Sanders has actually written and published.

* * *

Although Bernie Sanders has utterly defeated Donald Trump in the awkward misogynist moment category, I'm not sure this is really the type of evidence we should be using to evaluate who we want to lead our country. I think women should be most concerned, far and away, with Hillary Clinton's record of supporting and arming the regimes and, yes, terrorist groups, who are the very worst in the world when it comes to slaughtering, kidnapping, raping, and torturing women and girls.

Of course Hillary Clinton is quick to seize on any perceived slight against women on the part of Donald Trump. Claiming she "would love to debate him," she is clearly readying an entire deck of gender cards to play against him or any other male candidate who wins the GOP nomination. With both the neocon right-wing establishment media and the left "alternative" media behind her, she defines Trump as the "candidate who just seems to delight in insulting women every chance he gets."

And while Clinton and her campaign have been quick to jump on the bandwagon and apply the misogynist label to Trump, there is also evidence from his past that speaks otherwise. Of course nobody can deny that he is an unscripted, blunt-talking candidate who intentionally skirts the line of what is appropriate, almost baiting the left-wing with his perfect little soundbites, tailor-made for their daily sanctimonious outrage segment. Make no mistake, this is his chief tactic. Trump is the 140-character tweet and soundbite candidate, the first social media candidate. It doesn't burn cash, and it appears to be working very well for him.

It may have been a better idea to begin this book with the topic of women's rights, because it wasn't until I saw how exaggerated and, well, just plain wrong the media has become in trying to pin the sexist label on him, until I saw how desperate and overreaching *both sides* had become in their attempts to dismiss, to "disqualify" Trump with their ad hominem labels, that I started to wonder if maybe he wasn't quite the bad guy the media was so disingenuously insisting he was.

Trump's personal record of hiring and promoting women to the top spots in his business organization, in entrusting female executives with the highest levels of responsibility and then giving them the freedom and the power to succeed are unquestionably credentials of paramount importance for a president. They also put the lie to the contention that Trump can simply be written off as a sexist bigot, which is what Hillary Clinton and Fox News would both like us to do.

These accusations and the power of the media to sink any candidate with their derogatory labels don't work on Donald Trump for a single reason, more than any other. Thanks to reality television, the American people have actually had more than a glimpse into Donald Trump's spats with and insults against women AND men for quite some time, and he has proven beyond any shadow of a doubt that he's an equal opportunity destroyer.

Yes, of course, anyone who has watched more than a few hours of television in the last decade can point to numerous times when his decorum was less than presidential, but look what we've gotten so far from the political class who conduct themselves so decorously: professional liars who talk like saints and act like demons. At this point, I think most Americans would much rather elect an imperfect human being who is so down-to-earth that, although we might find some of his comments cringe-worthy, there's no doubt that we're getting the actual feed from inside his head, and not some rosy throw-away teleprompter script.

Imagine if we had a direct line to the inner thoughts of a Bush, a Cheney, an Obama, or a Clinton – I think we'd be getting a much different story than what's been coming out of their mouths. Of all of our recent executive branch leaders, really only Joe Biden has demonstrated this occasional tendency to accidentally connect his brain to his mouth, and the results are often quite telling.

* * *

Hillary Clinton's support for al-Qaeda and ISIS, not to mention Saudi Arabia which has the worst record on women's rights of any country in the world, is something that has had far more devastating consequences for women and girls than the bruised egos that have resulted from Donald Trump's big mouth. Iraq,

Libya, Syria – these were all countries where women had enjoyed, if not parity with men, substantial rights and freedoms in comparison with other countries in their respective regions. I don't think anyone would argue that these countries were paragons of human rights, but not too many people say that about the United States anymore, either. Especially not now that our record of supporting radical Islamic terrorists has been documented for posterity.

Hillary Clinton, with the help of her conciliatory rival Bernie Sanders, has managed to turn her support of al-Qaeda with arms funneled into Benghazi into some sort of theatrical partisan victory, in which she plays the stoic hero who refuses to divulge the secrets the evil Republicans tried to pry from her.

But let's look at what Benghazi really was: the toehold port city from which the CIA brought in enormous shipments of arms to supply and fund al-Qaeda in order to bring down Muammar Gaddafi, establishing a terrorist-controlled dictatorship that plunged the country – and the position of women within it – into a new dark age. With the arms and wealth they have been given by the US, its allies, and what has been taken from Gaddafi's armory, al-Qaeda has made alliances with like-minded groups like Boko Haram in Nigeria and al-Shabaab in Somalia, in turn providing them with the funding, weapons and aid they needed to grow into a major threat.

Your taxpayer dollars are hard at work fighting for women's rights, rest assured!

One of the favorite targets for the civilian massacres committed by these extremist Islamic terrorists, i.e. ISIS, al-Qaeda, al-Nusra, Boko Haram or any number of other evil groups Hillary Clinton's "progressive" foreign policy arms and protects, seems to be schools that have the audacity to teach female students. So it should have come as no surprise to Clinton and her boss when 270 girls were kidnapped by the same Boko Haram Islamist group in Nigeria who had directly benefited from the transfer of Libya into the hands of their terrorist allies. Clinton even personally led the effort to prevent Boko Haram from being designated a terrorist group over the objections of multiple intelligence agencies and elected representatives.

Ms. Clinton tried to position herself, as did Michelle Obama, as a leader in the effort to 'bring the girls back home.' It was a nice thought, but like a Band-Aid on a gangrenous open wound, it was far too little and far too late to undo her deal with the devil. More than 200 of the girls are still missing after over a year and a half, and although there has been a great deal of speculation about the girls being killed, enslaved, or perhaps still being held somewhere, nobody can say for certain what has happened to them. The ones who have escaped have told of horrific torture and rape, as well as threats against their families' lives if they failed to cooperate with Boko Haram.

At least progressives can count on the fact that Clinton still hasn't learned her lesson and intends to continue to press for regime change in Syria, so that the remaining population centers, like, say, Damascus, can too experience the joys of living under the Islamic State, where women's rights will be but a memory. Of course, all the young girls will look up to Hillary Clinton and be grateful for the liberation she's brought them, just like they are in Libya, Nigeria and Iraq.

Over and over again we hear stories like this. Unfortunately, the nearly 300 victims of this single kidnapping by Boko Haram are just a drop in the bucket when it comes to the atrocities the decisions of the Clinton/Obama team have caused to women and girls. Most recently, it was reported that an ISIS mortar attack killed nine girls and injured many more in the Syrian city of Deir el-Zour. It's hardly even news anymore when Islamists kill scores of innocent young women whose crime was going to school.

Women are executed, tortured and raped on a daily basis in the most barbaric of ways under Islamic

State rule, under the rule of al-Qaeda in the Islamic Maghreb in Libya, by Boko Haram and countless other al-Qaeda or Islamic State affiliates and splinter groups. Even knowing the consequences her actions have already had, Hillary Clinton transparently wants to extend their rule to new areas under the guise of fighting them. If I were to detail the many major and minor atrocities, offenses, discriminatory policies and abuses against women the terrorist groups that Ms. Clinton's State Department supported have carried out, it would require its own book. Indeed, many have been written – in blood.

It's no wonder the neoconservative death-cult wing of the Republican Party seems to have fallen in love with Hillary Clinton now that Trump is the GOP front-runner. Her policy of arming Islamic radicals to destabilize Assad's government simply continues *exactly* what the Bush administration had already begun doing in Syria, we now know from the Wikileaks cables.

* * *

I hope I've demonstrated so far that Donald Trump is not exactly the darling of the Republican establishment. His commanding lead in the GOP race for the White House is even more impressive when we consider the fact that he is *also* no starry-eyed born-again fanatic from the religious right. In the past, Republicans usually have had to choose between Eastern establishment candidates like the Bushes and the Romneys and religious conservatives like Huckabee, although every once in a while a celebrity candidate who is already popular outside of politics will bridge the divide, like a Reagan or a Schwarzenegger. Or a Trump.

As I looked further into the attacks that were being leveled against Trump, I found that while the left and their niche publications were dead-set on the idea that Trump was an arch-conservative, sexist, racist, basically any label they can pull out and use with as little thought or effort as possible (even the word "fascist" was being thrown around irresponsibly), a few conservatives like Glenn Beck were trying to smear him as a "liberal," or even – horrors! – a "progressive."

Donald Trump has been a supporter of a woman's right to choose to have an abortion, albeit reluctantly, and although he has made a point of stating that he is now pro-life, he is still being attacked as pro-choice by the Republican establishment. Like Mitt Romney who claimed to be pro-choice and then switched his views to garner the support of the GOP base, Trump has faced a great deal of criticism for his past views, and his ingenuity in coming up with ways to be pro-life and yet still support a woman's right to choose has even earned him the praise of Planned Parenthood.

Hold the phone! Planned Parenthood actually *officially* issued a statement praising Donald Trump's "pro-life" position? Well, Trump is nobody's fool, and as Planned Parenthood's statement points out, he knows how to make a deal that will satisfy both sides of the debate better than any other candidate in the race. Although he insists he will defund Planned Parenthood if they continue to do abortions, placating pro-life members of his party, he has long stated that he will continue to fund the other operations that the organization does to help women.

Well – guess what? This is how the law stands now. Federal funding for Planned Parenthood is not allowed to go to abortions as it is, so Trump's position essentially represents no change from what we have now. It is a wise compromise.

If we give him the chance, Donald Trump displays a unique ability to unite America around a compromise that satisfies two highly contentious sides, allowing us to move aside one of those most insidious roadblocks to progress – the "wedge issues" they use to divide us into political parties who engage in a theatrical pageantry of difference on these select issues, so that we will be so blinded with rage that we won't recognize that we all agree on more basic issues, like not trying to topple more-or-less benevolent dictator after more-or-less benevolent dictator in order to replace them with Chef Bush or Chef Obama's caliphate *du jour*.

Women are right to be worried about a Republican president, but I think it's clear women can trust Donald Trump not to legislate their rights away. Of course he has to move toward the right to win the GOP nomination in the primary season; that's how the game works, and how many times have we heard (and seen) that Trump plays to win?

And yes, he has hardened his position a bit toward Planned Parenthood, but let's face it: those hidden camera videos that have been coming out showing what has occasionally gone on in Planned Parenthood have been more than a little shocking. Those of us who do support reproductive rights should admit, to ourselves and to our political opponents, that we can't support everything our political allies may do just because we're on the same "team." There is room for compromise and some decorum, and Donald Trump has managed to carve out a space of agreement, and both sides would be wise not to push him too far in either direction. They may only end up hurting their own side.

Because if he wins the Republican nominating process, Trump will then have to move his rhetoric toward the center to win over undecided voters, independents, assorted riff-raff and maybe even, if I may be so bold, some of the progressive wing of the Democratic Party. But his core positions needn't be altered, many of which have changed less in the past few decades than it may appear, in order to win America over to his side.

Not if we recognize the chance we have to break the cycle of lies we've been stuck in for far too long. Bernie Sanders is wrong – the women of the world aren't the subservient, submissive, masochistic slaves of the war machine who just want to be raped, politically, spiritually and physically, by the crass manipulation of a two-party system whose specialty is tag-team mass murder. I hope women *and* men in the US won't forget the women, girls, and their families in Libya, in Syria, in Iraq, in Nigeria, who have died or are still suffering as a result of the insanity of our schizophrenic foreign policy.

NO, WE COULDN'T. MAYBE A TRUMP CAN?

During Barack Obama's first 100 days in office, he had so much going for him: tremendous goodwill, a Democratic House and Senate, the entire world was behind him and he could have accomplished nearly anything. Instead, his administration quickly sat down at the global chessboard and continued the game exactly where Bush left off.

There are so many ways in which progressives have been betrayed for their support of Barack Obama, but perhaps one of the most obvious and hypocritical is the war on weed. Obama hasn't just tried marijuana, he was a real stoner back in the day with his "Choom Gang" buddies. Despite the fact that over 50% of Americans now favor legalization of marijuana even for recreational use, and despite the fact that the voluminous scientific evidence supporting medical marijuana is now unassailable, Obama hasn't even taken the simple step that he could take with one swipe of his pen: to reclassify marijuana from Schedule I (the most dangerous drugs with no medical use like heroin, LSD – and *hemp*?) to *at least* Schedule III (highly addictive and dangerous drugs that may have a medical use and therefore can be prescribed). Patients have been offered pharmaceutical synthetics and extracts, but they often complain these are less effective, too potent psychoactively, and in general not as good as the simple plant, just as Jah made it.

The number of honest, hard-working Americans who have been imprisoned for mere marijuana "crimes" is staggering. Bill Clinton, the first conductor of this drug war hypocrisy train who famously forgot to inhale, had no problem with his prison system inhaling nonviolent drug offenders at a massively increased rate. To his credit, he apologized earlier this year for imprisoning an entire generation of young people who were into Pearl Jam and Snoop Dogg, but it doesn't really matter now, does it? Nonviolent, disproportionately minority prisoners will never get back the lifetimes stolen from them by

Clinton's need to look like he was tough on pot, despite having played the saxophone.

It's like Barney Frank putting his name on Dodd-Frank *after* he gives away the store. That bill was supposed to prevent any more bailouts after the fact, but I bet they had a good laugh about that up on the Hill with Hank Paulson. And now the law has been gutted and taxpayers are once again potentially on the hook for trillions in gambling debts incurred by too-big-to-jail banks. Barney Frank gets to hand over the keys to the treasury and satisfy the powers who have so graciously allowed him to serve, and then they let him do a little photo op and pose as a cop instead of the robber he is.

Likewise, Obama has increased federal raids on medical marijuana growers and dispensaries, outspending and out-incarcerating the Bush administration. At the same time, raising the hypocritical stakes even higher, Obama's Attorney General Eric Holder lied condescendingly to Congress, telling them that his Justice Department *wasn't* raiding medical marijuana facilities, only those who "took advantage" of the many different state medical marijuana laws. Inside this nebulous concept of 'taking advantage,' there is evidently a vast amount of room for interpretation, because they had, under the color of law, administratively redefined many of those compliant with their state's laws as criminals and were busily carting them off to prison.

* * *

This is only one of many issues where the American people deserved better from Obama and from Mr. Clinton. We progressives have to learn a tough lesson: paradoxically, many of the things that we want done can only be done, for reasons of pure political logistics, by a Republican. A Democratic president would have to fight Republicans tooth and nail for every tiny move in a progressive direction, but if the same proposals that Democrats want were to come from a Republican president – why, that's a whole different ballgame now, isn't it? I'm not saying Nixon is a wonderful example to follow, but many of the things he accomplished, like expanding Social Security and Medicare, were made possible by the fact that they were coming from a conservative.

Please don't misunderstand me. I'm certainly not arguing that, as a general rule, we should elect Republicans if we want Democratic policies and vice versa. If you elect a Bush, that's exactly what you're going to get. But what if a Republican president, one who didn't put allegiance to his party first, but to the American people, were to suggest some of the things that we progressives have been demanding for far too long? That might be a horse, or rather an elephant, of a different color.

Donald Trump has, in the past, claimed to support the full legalization of all drugs, though he also claims to have never had so much as a cup of coffee, nor a cigarette or a drink of alcohol. He may well be the most drug-free person in America. Obviously he's had to back off from his position of total legalization, but he remains "100%" in support of medical marijuana, and also recognizes the right of states like Colorado, Washington, Oregon, Alaska (and probably others soon, perhaps California in 2016) to legalize and tax marijuana for recreational use. If the Republican Party under Trump's leadership can join with progressive Democrats, we might see the first major thawing of federal marijuana laws since the hemp plant was outlawed in 1937, disguised using the racist pejorative "marihuana" to associate it with Mexican immigrants.

Hillary Clinton unfortunately seems determined to repeat the mistakes her husband made and lock up a whole new generation of disproportionately minority marijuana "offenders." Far from coming to terms with the states which have legalized and taxed marijuana for adults, Clinton is still drudging up the long-outdated claim that the scientific evidence for medical marijuana still isn't in yet, saying only a month ago that "we haven't done any research."

In fact, the evidence has been in for quite some time, at least since the 1999 release of the National Academy of Sciences' Institute of Medicine report during her husband's tenure in the White House. Our Founding Fathers would weep if they knew we ruined so many lives over the hemp plants they revered as the agricultural backbone of this nation.

We've certainly given the Democrats enough chances to do something about locking up young people and ruining families over one of the plants that built this country, and guess what happened? No, they couldn't. Maybe a Trump can?

* * *

And what about single-payer health care? Donald Trump had been in favor of it for a very long time. Obamacare, like the medical insurance industry who wrote it, is a fraud perpetrated on the American people. If we are going to provide everyone with health care and actually be able to afford it, we have to cut out the middleman, i.e. the medical insurance industry itself, which we simply do not need. As a businessman, undoubtedly the cost savings that come from integration is a topic Trump is well versed in. He hasn't released his health plan yet. But if he is even considering anything resembling single-payer health care, he would be wise to wait until after he has won the nomination to unveil it – even though it could ultimately win him the general election.

When Trump briefly toyed with the idea of running for president in the 2000 election, he sounded very much like he was backing a single-payer universal health care system like Canada has, and it's not exactly clear how different his views are today. He still supports universal health care, and although he demures that much of it will be private, he is still very clearly in favor of the poorest being guaranteed health care that the government will pay for – hardly your typical Republican who is only willing to open the government coffers for massive corporate subsidies, bailouts and welfare for the rich! If he can drag Republicans over to some of his positions, isn't that worth the price of admission alone?

What Trump has said about his health care plan is promising, but it's not clear yet how it differs from the Romney/Obama healthcare exchange approach. Writing in *Crippled America*, Trump makes one specific proposal to allow for more competition between insurance companies, while at the same time he does unfortunately argue against a larger role for government in health care.

It does seem that middle-class America has been most hurt by Obamacare, even though it has been good for many less well-off Americans, so it does make sense that Trump's fixes would focus on the segment of the population who actually has to purchase health insurance under the plan.

But if he is elected, he might just have the ability to work out a much better deal for American health care, and better yet, the Republicans won't be able to score political points by opposing it. One thing is for certain: if Donald Trump is elected president, single-payer (or something closer to it than Obamacare) would have a much better chance of passing than if Bernie Sanders were in office, simply because Republicans will be able to go along with it if Trump does it. Those are just the facts.

Trump has also long been an advocate for shoring up Social Security and preventing the funds from being misused, similar to Al Gore's famous "lockbox" quote. In *The America we Deserve*, Trump even used the same word, "lock-box," to describe his proposal to segregate Social Security funds from the government's general fund. Our seniors who have paid into the system, and those who are paying in now, deserve no less – but other Republicans and their donors (who always seem to have their hands out) have very different ideas about what to do with your money.

Besides the ones we've already mentioned – stopping war/interventionism, actually fighting terrorists, reducing illegal immigration to help all American workers, standing up for women's rights without being beholden to terrorists or to Saudi Arabia and other repressive regimes, not endangering reproductive rights, preventing the incarceration of nonviolent weed "criminals," universal health care, and saving Social Security/SSI – there are many other issues on which Trump's positions are similar to, or better than, the positions of the Democratic candidates.

I certainly don't want to make it seem like any particular issue is less important, because I know that for some people who are most affected, it could be the most important thing in the world. I've chosen the topics for more in-depth discussion in the previous chapters based on what the media has been talking about and trying to answer the smears that have been made against Mr. Trump first. Other issues I haven't touched on as much because they have not been as contentious, but that doesn't mean they aren't crucial to progressives.

For example, it would be an absolute deal-breaker for me if Donald Trump supported outlawing same-sex marriage by constitutional amendment as many of his Republican rivals would like to do. That is an ill-conceived idea that would never work. With his calculated moderate stance, Trump has received the praise of the Log Cabin Republicans and he has taken heat from evangelicals for his declaration that the court's recent decision has settled the issue once and for all.

* * *

I have long been suspicious of the big moneyed interests who have been steering our focus away from the biggest environmental concerns of our age: pollution, extinction, deforestation, crimes like Fukushima or the BP oil spill which could inconvenience the pocketbooks of investors. They've written a new songbook for environmentalists to sing, and this choir gets paid. They've composed a rousing chorus of "blame humanity," but individual corporate actors find themselves gleefully written out of the musical. The name of the show is Global Warming, starring Cap-and-Trade. It's being used to implement global carbon trading schemes, similar to Enron, to the benefit of investment banks.

Now, many of the solutions proposed to this, I'm sorry to say, *over-hyped* issue are in and of themselves good ideas: solar/wind power, less dependence on fossil fuels, recycling/reusing, planting trees, etc. But the idea that carbon emissions are the be-all-end-all of our environmental problems is extremely dangerous. We are ignoring important problems like the fact that much of our recyclable waste is not actually being recycled, an infrastructure that encourages individual transportation using fossil fuels, fracking, GMOs, pesticides/herbicides or the Great Pacific Garbage Patch. Unfortunately it's easy to see where the funding is, what topics are going to get journalists and academics published, and where the focus will continue to be: trapped in the safe-space greenhouse of hot-air research.

When Donald Trump insults the very idea of global warming, it's not as bad as it might sound. If you still think New York City is going to end up underwater and you wake up screaming in the night feeling the waves rushing over your bedsheets, then maybe this particular argument won't convince you. But if we put aside the need for Goldman Sachs to make bazillions of dollars for one moment, and if we manage to elect a president who hasn't taken ungodly sums from every single environmental offender in the known universe, we might actually be able to address some of our less illusory environmental concerns.

WORSE THAN WE THOUGHT?

Even as I write this, new, even more damning information has come to light about the Obama administration's support for ISIS in the form of an article by Pulitzer Prize-winning journalist Seymour Hersh, "Military to Military," in the *London Review of Books*. If we hadn't just experienced the exact same type of treasonous behavior on the part of the Bush administration, what he writes would simply be beyond belief.

Luckily for the United States and really for all of humanity, the Pentagon's Joint Chiefs of Staff made the decision to share intelligence with allies that ultimately sabotaged Obama's support of ISIS, according to Hersh.

I know we've all heard the joke that "military intelligence" is an oxymoron, but in this case it seems that the military was acting in a far more intelligent fashion than its civilian leadership, if Seymour Hersh's story is to be believed. I have no reason to doubt the story's veracity, as his principal sources are very highly placed and at least one, Defense Intelligence Agency director Lt. General Michael Flynn, has gone on record backing up the allegations in the article. Judging by the silence of the mass media regarding the revelations contained in the story, they can't or won't allow the public to know how badly we have been deceived – which has the incidental benefit of allowing their talking heads to keep right on deceiving us.

Although the wars we have fought since 9/11 have apparently only used the fight against terrorism as a pretext for other, mysterious geopolitical objectives, it seems our nation's military has taken it upon themselves to make just the shift that Trump had already called for fifteen years ago, transitioning from fighting wars to fighting terror, out of sheer sanity and pragmatic necessity.

Hersh's article states that is the "view" of "some of the most senior officers on the Pentagon's Joint Staff" that

"Obama is captive to Cold War thinking about Russia and China, and hasn't adjusted his stance on Syria to the fact both countries share Washington's anxiety about the spread of terrorism in and beyond Syria." Instead of fighting ISIS, Hersh writes, the Obama administration's "fixation" is on "Assad's primary ally, Vladimir Putin."

Prior to Obama's push for war in Syria, the Joint Chiefs produced a "bleak" intelligence assessment which stated categorically that "there was no viable 'moderate' opposition to Assad, and the US was arming extremists" while the Defense Intelligence Agency "sent a constant stream of warnings to the civilian leadership about the dire consequences of toppling Assad."

Over the objection of his own military, Obama continued the policy of transferring weapons from Libya to Syria, and then from Turkey to Syria. One who objected particularly strongly to Obama's refusal to target ISIS was Lt. General Michael Flynn, who was in charge of the DIA at the time. He is quoted in Hersh's article with the following shocking statement:

> *If the American public saw the intelligence we were producing daily, at the most sensitive level, they would go ballistic.*

The Obama administration knew exactly what they were doing, and according to Flynn, they made a "willful" decision to support ISIS instead of listening to their own military's warnings.

What the military decided to do was truly nothing less than brilliant. Because the Pentagon leaders felt that any "direct challenge" to Obama's policy of arming ISIS would have "zero chance of success," Hersh writes, they came up with a strategy of sharing the intelligence they had on ISIS with the Syrian government via Germany, Israel, and Russia, which would then allow for the Syrian government, increasingly with the help of the Russian military, to do what the US military was being shamefully prevented from doing: to strike ISIS terrorist targets using very accurate American intelligence.

It's *no wonder* then, that we Americans cheered the Russians finally doing something about ISIS, even as the media and the White House cried foul – it was our own military who brought them in as Assad's advisers in the first place! One of the four preconditions the Joint Chiefs placed on intelligence sharing with Syria was the introduction of "Russian and other outside military advisers."

It seems pretty clear that our own military felt supporting ISIS terrorists was so treasonous that they trusted the Kremlin more than the White House. It's nice to know that Putin, who obviously knew the score the entire time, acted rationally and did only what was morally necessary, and he did it knowing full well that the US military wanted it done, even though their hands were tied. It was US intelligence that made the Russian bombing campaign so successful, it seems.

And that's why Vladimir Putin and Donald Trump have such mutual respect, because they're on the same side in this battle, as are the American and Russian people. We all want a peace free from terrorism, but also free from the interventionist wars that create terrorists and use them. Except for a very tiny minority who think they can get away with lying forever, simply because it's worked for them so far.

Already in 1999, Donald Trump was arguing very forcefully that our nation's defensive strategy needed to shift from an outdated Cold War mentality that focuses on large state actors like Russia and China to guarding our nation against asymmetric warfare – in other words, he was talking about the threat of terrorism.

Since the 9/11 attacks, Trump's views have become the norm on a rhetorical level, but not in actual practice. I'm asking you to consider putting an end to this cycle of abuse and deception of the American population, and I submit to you that supporting Donald Trump in this election is the only possible chance we have of doing so.

* * *

I had planned at this point to compare Donald Trump's statements against the Iraq War with Hillary Clinton's statements in support of it. It would be a nice, safe way to prove my point and tie a little bow on top of my argument.

There's only one problem. I know what you're thinking – if you're against war, then you should support Bernie Sanders instead of Donald Trump. I'm sorry to have to take your comfort blanket away, progressives. I know all you Bernie Sanders supporters want to "keep it positive, bro," but I'm hardly the first one to say this: your makeshift progressive icon isn't quite the Ben & Jerry's-eating peacenik you think he is. And when lives are at stake, it's selfish and irresponsible to put your need to continue the adolescent project of constructing a really hip identity first and try to stand in the way of a someone who actually has a chance of reigning in the insane mass murder they call "regime change" that *both* parties have been guilty of for a long, long time. Including Bernie Sanders.

In 1999, after Senator Bernie Sanders voted for airstrikes in Yugoslavia that killed many hundreds of civilians, one of the Senator's staff, Jeremy Brecher, resigned over the unnecessary war. In his resignation letter, Brecher wrote that Sanders' and Clinton's war was characterized by "not just collateral damage but the deliberate selection of civilian targets, including residential neighborhoods, auto factories, broadcasting stations, and hydro-electric power plants."

Donald Trump too complained about the war in Yugoslavia in *The America we Deserve*, using it as an example of an unnecessary war, as opposed to a targeted strike that would take out weapons or terrorist facilities that truly threaten America, in this case a North Korean nuclear facility:

> *Doesn't it make at least as much sense to take out these truly threatening facilities as it does to blow up buildings and bridges in downtown Belgrade, Yugoslavia? It would be much smarter to remove a potential threat to this country than to get involved in a civil war in the Balkans, which posed no threat whatsoever to our national security.*

Trump's test of whether a war would be justified, only in the case of a threat to our national security, is hard to argue with. The problem is not to be found in any high-minded philosophical ideal that we can nitpick. The problem is very simple, unfortunately. Presidents have been lying to us about national security for a long time.

The Bush administration's Iraq War was carried out under false pretenses. Weapons of mass destruction and links to al-Qaeda have all proven to be nothing more than Dick Cheney's fairy tales. And now in Syria, the geopolitical purpose of the war has long been at odds with the fabricated story that we are going after our own secret army of people who hate us. Nothing has changed. Regime change seems to be the goal in and of itself.

And for what? Are these better places now for all the lives it's cost?

When Trump talks about having a "strong" country again, I think it's important to note that what he means by "strength" might be a little different from the chicken-hawk's definition. Trump wants the United States to have the strongest military in the world instead of the most overextended one.

"It will be so powerful that I don't think we're ever going to have to use it," he says.

Imagine that – a Department of Defense that actually gets to focus on defense. Our military has been broken by unwinnable wars that it must fight blindfolded with one hand tied behind its back, even as the White House switches sides and runs "rat lines" to supply the bad guys. Trump is offering us the different path forward, the path to peace, that we thought we were going to get from Obama.

* * *

Since you've been kind enough to read this book through to the end, I hope you've at least been informed and may even have agreed with some of the things you've read. But I can only imagine the conversations you might be having with friends and loved ones who have been convinced by the media that Donald Trump is the worst person on the face of this earth and that anyone who supports him is sexist, racist, or whatever insult they can get their lips around.

For a social animal like the human, the fear of ostracism is one of our greatest fears. We want to belong, to fit in and be accepted, and the media is now using that fear of ostracism against us – that's why the simple ad hominem dismissals of Trump and his supporters as racist, sexist, bigoted, etc. are so effective. Nobody wants to be labeled any of these because they're really all stand-ins for the word "crazy," with all of the accompanying baggage of not really being a valid member of society.

These rhetorical weapons of mass destruction that the media have used to carpet bomb the Trump campaign have been accepted uncritically by much of the left and some of the right. While many of us profess to be independent-minded voters who are well aware that the media lies to us (and I do think it's true that Americans are becoming less and less enamored with both political parties), we are still surrounded by people who have a conditioned, visceral hatred of Donald Trump and his supporters. The force of peer pressure can be tremendous – nobody wants to become an object of ridicule to their friends, their peers, their coworkers. If you're a progressive, you're probably also surrounded by like-minded people in your circle of friends as well, and I feel your pain. The all-out drive to condemn Trump as some kind of monster in the media has created a terrible atmosphere that is designed to ensure that progressives like us don't give him a second look, and to intimidate those who do support Trump so that they will be afraid to say so.

I think it's clear Donald Trump isn't the monster you and your friends have been told he is. The only people who should really be afraid of Trump being elected are corporate special interests, terrorists, and those in Washington who have supported them clandestinely. He may be tough and he certainly does say derogatory things, but what we've been getting from the Democrats *and* the Republicans is nothing less than treason. We need a tough guy who is on our side for once, not one who is going to be tough on the American people, but tough on those who have been devastating our economy by putting their (increasingly foreign) backers first and running up nearly unpayable bills with mindless invasions and wars.

For too long, the promises voters have been made by politicians have melted away like they were painted by Salvador Dali. But I believe Donald Trump possesses a genuine desire to serve the American people first and a steadfast determination (not to mention the exceptionally rare financial ability) to retain the independence that will allow him to do so.

Who thought the first thing Obama would do when he got into office was hand over the keys to the treasury to the banks? Did anyone see that coming? I bet his Wall Street donors and their lobbyists did. They're counting on being able to scare us into foreclosing on ourselves, to sell our hope for a better country at a bargain price, like they've always been able to do before.

I don't think the banks are going to be a match for Donald Trump.

During the 1980s farm crisis, after three consecutive years of drought and three years of mortgages, a Georgia farmer tried to save his family's farm from foreclosure by committing suicide, hoping to pay off his mortgage with the proceeds from his life insurance. Even more tragically, he wasn't aware that life insurance policies generally don't cover suicide, and the bank was going to get the farm anyway.

Who came to his widow's rescue? A wealthy New Yorker named Donald Trump pledged his own money and went on TV with her to raise money and awareness of the plight of farmers in her family's situation, and together they saved the family's farm.

But he didn't do it by playing nice.

In his book *The Art of the Deal*, Trump describes how he threatened the bank, and how his trademark off-the-cuff, no-nonsense bravado paid off for the widow and her family:

> *I called [the bank] and got some vice president on the line. I explained that I was a businessman from New York, and that I was interested in helping Mrs. Hill. He told me he was sorry, but that it was too late. They were going to auction off the farm, he said, and "nothing or no one is going to stop it."*
>
> *That really got me going. I said to the guy: "You listen to me. If you do foreclose, I'll personally bring a lawsuit for murder against you and your bank, on the grounds that you harassed Mrs. Hill's husband to his death." All of a sudden the bank officer sounded very nervous and said he'd get right back to me.*
>
> *Sometimes it pays to be a little wild. An hour later I got a call back from the banker, and he said, "Don't worry, we're going to work it out, Mr. Trump."*

Ultimately, he got the bank to make a deal. Trump's ability to negotiate from a position of strength where all others see is hopelessness is exactly what our country needs. The American people, the least among us most of all, need someone with Trump's backbone to negotiate on our behalf.

Trump didn't just write *The Art of the Deal*, he followed it up with *The Art of the Comeback*. At his low point, after the bottom fell out of the real estate market a few decades ago, Trump found himself $900 million dollars in debt. Not only did he not file for personal bankruptcy even though much of this debt was in the form of personal guarantees, he made it back plus many billions more. If America's going to make a comeback from the brink of debt and endless war without complete collapse, and it's reasonable to wonder if that's even possible, then Trump is quite probably the only one who can do it.

* * *

The other candidates and the media are trying to brand Donald Trump as the candidate of "fear." But that's because they want you to be afraid, afraid that it would be irresponsible to loosen the grasp of the myriad special interests who all have a stake in the establishment candidates. The Democratic Party is a finely-tuned machine, designed to absorb the energy of progressives while suppressing their progressive values within the party, and that's why Bernie Sanders' endorsement of Hillary Clinton is a foregone conclusion. He has no chance whatsoever.

The establishment wing of the Republican Party is also particularly well-supplied with dirty tricks, as we all know, but it's tough to rig an election when it's a blowout. That's why we see the daily onslaught of attack after attack from an increasingly desperate corporate media, and the alternative media falls right into lock-step with the parade of politically correct peacocks.

When Trump just keeps giving them more and more "wild" soundbites on which to feed, instead of apologizing and retreating with his tail between his legs for the last ten or twenty, it's like he's hacked into some hidden infinite loop flaw in the media's programming and suddenly all you hear on the television and all you see on the internet is Donald Trump.

We progressives are going to have to be a little wild, too, if we expect to be taken seriously. The Democrats think they can pat us on the head and send us on our way while they foreclose on our dreams of a better world, and, so far, they've been right.

But the two-party monopoly on power has brought us to the brink of destruction, and as they hold us by the legs, dangling over the precipice, they tell us not to give in to "fear" and vote for Donald Trump. They claim that the terrorists will somehow "win" if we vote for the one candidate who will actually fight them. They claim we'll be giving in to racism instead of stopping their genocide. They'll claim that day is night and night is day, they'll say whatever they can possibly think of to hold onto their grip on power.

Do your own research before you trust the media, and that includes much of the so-called "alternative" media, which is often just as controlled, if not more so, than the mainstream media.

The words of a liar are always easy on the ear. If you want more highly palatable drivel with a hidden side order of complete betrayal and mass murder, vote for a Jeb Bush or a Hillary Clinton. It doesn't really matter which.

But if you don't want to waste what may well be America's last chance to vote in a president who truly does not represent the special interests nor the foreign policy interventionists to whom America's blood, sweat and tears mean nothing, then it may be time for us progressives to grow up a little bit and reject the simplistic manipulation of our values for evil.

The world is counting on us to do the right thing. I pray that we recognize what that is.